HISTORY THROUGH
NewspApErs

19th CENTURY REFORM

Nathaniel Harris

HODDER
Wayland

an imprint of Hodder Children's Books

Produced for Hodder Wayland by
Discovery Books Ltd
Unit 3, 37 Watling Street, Leintwardine, Shropshire SY7 0LW

First published in 2002 by Hodder Wayland, an imprint of Hodder Children's Books

British Library Cataloguing in Publication Data
Harris, Nathaniel, 1937-
Nineteenth century reform. – (History through newspapers)
1.Great Britain – Social conditions – 19th century –
Sources – Juvenile literature 2.Great Britain – Social
conditions – 19th century – Press coverage – Juvenile
literature 3. Great Britain – Politics and government – 19th
century – Sources – Juvenile literature 4.Great Britain –
Politics and government – 19th century – Press coverage –
Juvenile literature
I.Title
941'.081
ISBN 0750241853

Printed and bound in Italy by G. Canale

Designer: Ian Winton
Cover design: Claire Bond
Series editors: Jane Tyler and Kathryn Walker
Picture research: Rachel Tisdale

learn.co.uk is a trade mark of Guardian Education Interactive Limited
and is used under license

Hodder Children's Books would like to thank the following for the loan of their material:
The Art Archive: Cover; Copyright in the newspaper extracts on pages 10, 14, 22, 26, 28 © *Learnthings
Limited* and *Guardian Newspapers Limited*; **Hulton Getty:** pages 6-7, 9, 13, 19, 25, 27, 29; **Mary Evans Picture
Library:** pages 4, 5, 11, 15, 17, 20-21, 23.

The website addresses (URLs) included in this book were valid at the time of going to press. However,
because of the nature of the Internet, it is possible that some addresses may have changed, or sites may have
changed or closed down since publication. While the author and Publisher regret any inconvenience this may
cause readers, no responsibility for any such changes can be accepted by either the author or the Publisher.

Hodder Children's Books
A division of Hodder Headline Limited
338 Euston Road
London NW1 3BH

CONTENTS

The Age of Reform   4

The Peterloo Massacre   6

The Reform Bill Crisis   8

Freeing the Slaves   10

Reforming the Boroughs   12

The Chartist Movement   14

Reform of the Workplace   16

Into the Workhouse   18

The Free Trade Era   20

Education for the Masses   22

The Nation's Health   24

New Political Reforms   26

Women's Rights   28

Timeline   30

Glossary   30

Resources   31

Index   32

THE AGE OF REFORM

ABOUT THIS BOOK

This book presents a series of extracts from 19th-century British newspapers. A range of sources is used so that different opinions are represented. Each article deals with conditions that needed to be changed, or with a **reforming movement** or **Act** of Parliament. On the same double page you will find key background information and a separate 'Evaluation' panel which explains difficult points in the extract and suggests how to approach it as a piece of historical evidence. For example, it asks whether the statements in the extracts are reliable and unbiased.

As newspapers appear daily or weekly, they deal with issues and events as they happen. To make money, they must sell in large numbers – which means that their contents must please their regular readers. So newspaper articles provide evidence about readers' opinions and attitudes.

Furthermore, each newspaper generally tries to attract particular groups of readers. It wants to please them, but also tries to keep or win their support for its policies. So a newspaper also tells us something about the ideas and aims of its owners and editors.

The 19th century was a great age of **reform**, because far-sighted people realized that reforms of many kinds were urgently needed. Most of the problems and abuses of the period were the effects of social and economic change. Such change was not new, but from the late 18th century it took place at an uncontrollable, breakneck speed, transforming Britain within a few generations from a mainly agricultural country to the industrial 'Workshop of the World'.

The transformation is described as the Industrial Revolution. Its visible results were factory-filled landscapes, spectacular new machines such as steam engines and steamships,

A traditional scene: Birmingham in the West Midlands around 1800. Though some manufacturing was already going on here, it is still a country place.

Commercial centre: Birmingham in 1840, a huge new city. Its offices, factories, warehouses and slums lay at the heart of a great manufacturing region.

huge engineering projects such as railways, and new cities such as Birmingham and Manchester. Industry and business created important new social groups. Among the better-off, a middle class of factory owners and businessmen grew up beside the traditional landowning classes. Less well-off were the masses of working people who became concentrated in the factories and towns. Their labour created immense wealth for the factory owners, but they suffered from terrible social evils – poverty and unemployment, child labour, long hours of work, filthy living conditions, polluted cities, and **epidemic diseases**.

Nobody had intended this to happen. The change was so sudden, and the upheaval so great, that the traditional rulers had little idea of how to cope with them. But gradually, against strong resistance, the need for reform was recognized – reform of the out-of-date political system, economic reforms, and reforms to check and control the worst social evils. These, and their reflection in the newspapers of the day, are described in the pages that follow.

Political Parties

On several occasions, 19th-century political parties changed their names and adopted new policies. This can make it hard to sort out who supported or opposed a specific reform.

Early in the century, Tory governments opposed any change in the voting system. They were opposed by the Whigs, who favoured limited reform, and the Radicals, who wanted more far-reaching changes. After 1832, when the Whigs finally achieved their aims, the Tories were reorganized by Sir Robert Peel into the Conservative Party (but 'Tory' stuck as a nickname, still used today). The Conservatives accepted the Whig reforms and, although cautious in their attitude to change, passed reforms of their own in the 1840s.

In 1846 the Conservatives split on the issue of **Free Trade** (page 20), and party groupings were often confused until 1868. Then Whigs, Radicals and some others fused into the Liberal Party. After this, Liberal and Conservative remained the two great political opponents until the rise of the Labour Party in the 20th century.

THE PETERLOO MASSACRE

In 1815 Britain emerged triumphant from long wars with France, which ended with the Duke of Wellington's victory over Napoleon at Waterloo. The war had been a strain on the economy, and peace brought further problems. The Industrial Revolution was already leading to the replacement of craftsmen with machines, which caused unemployment and hardship. With peace, businesses such as arms factories were suddenly no longer profitable, and ex-soldiers and sailors became jobless. Consequently there was widespread discontent.

Britain was governed by the Tory Party, which mainly represented the wealthy, landowning class; few people had the right to vote, and in practice elections were controlled by the upper class. The Tory government was alarmed by marches of the unemployed, and by mass meetings demanding that more people should have the right to vote. The government's response was to pass harsher laws, for example suspending *habeas corpus* – the right of people who had been arrested to demand a trial. Any opposition to authority was liable to be put down by force.

EXPRESS FROM MANCHESTER

Dispersal of reform meeting at Manchester by a military force

The **Yeomanry** Cavalry were seen advancing in a rapid trot to the area ... After a moment's pause, the cavalry drew their swords, and brandished them fiercely in the air; upon which Hunt and Johnson [another radical leader] desired the multitude to give three cheers, to show the military that they were not to be daunted. ... The Manchester Yeoman cavalry rode into the mob which gave way before them, and directed their course to the cart from where Hunt was speaking. Not a brickbat [missile] was thrown at them – not a pistol was fired during this period: all was quiet and orderly. ... As soon as Hunt and Johnson had jumped from the waggon [under arrest], a cry was made by the cavalry, 'Have at their flags'. In consequence, they immediately dashed not only at the flags which were in the waggon, but those which were posted among the crowd, cutting most indiscriminately to the right and left in order to get at them. This set the people running in all directions, and it was not until this act had been committed that any brickbats were hurled at the military. From that moment the Manchester Yeoman cavalry lost all command of temper.

On 16 August 1819, a great demonstration was held in St Peter's Fields, Manchester, to demand voting rights. At least 60,000 people gathered to hear the radical leader, Henry **'Orator'** Hunt. It was a peaceful occasion, attended by many women and children.

(left) An eye-witness account of Peterloo from *The Times* of 19 August 1819.

Evaluation

This is an eye-witness report, though the author, John Tyas, writes, in the style of the time, that the cavalry 'were seen'. He certainly saw them himself, since he had managed to get a place in the waggon used by Hunt and other radical leaders. Tyas worked for *The Times*, the only national newspaper to send a reporter to the meeting. Though Tyas disliked the radicals and what he called 'the mob', his account made it clear that the meeting was peaceful and that the Yeomanry were the attackers.

Communications were slow, and descriptions of Peterloo by Tyas and others only appeared in *The Times* three days after the massacre. Tyas's account was delayed because he was among those arrested at St Peter's Fields, but it was a scoop for *The Times*. The paper became a major political influence and, previously conservative, championed **reform**.

The suspension dots [...] which appear in the newspaper articles used in this book indicate where portions of the original text have been omitted. Also, not all 19th-century newspaper articles carried headlines, so some of the headlines you see in this book were put in by the author.

Then the local **magistrates** ordered the Yeomanry to arrest Hunt and break up the meeting. The Yeomanry – volunteer cavalrymen (armed horsemen) from the better-off classes – drew their swords, and in the massacre which followed, 11 people were killed and over 400 injured.

Historians still argue about whether the cavalrymen acted deliberately or through panic, and whether the government was behind the violence. Nicknamed 'Peterloo' as a mocking reference to the battle of Waterloo, the massacre caused widespread outrage but failed to change the government's policy.

The massacre: swords drawn, the Yeomanry ride down the crowd while the platform speakers look helplessly on.

THE REFORM BILL CRISIS

In 1830 a Whig government took office, determined to **reform** the way the **House of Commons** was elected. This had hardly changed since the 17th century. Most boroughs (towns) and all of the counties elected two MPs, even though counties were of very different sizes. In most places, men had to possess some property to have the right to vote. But the amount required varied enormously in the boroughs, so that a place might have a handful of electors or thousands of them.

In practice, influential landlords had controlled the system and competed for political office. But by the 19th century, the Industrial Revolution had created great cities, such as Birmingham, Manchester and Leeds, which had not existed earlier and had no right to elect MPs. Many boroughs that did have this right had grown smaller and contained only a few voters (like the seven at deserted Old Sarum in Wiltshire), who were easily bribed or bullied; such places were known as 'rotten boroughs'.

BEAT THE DUKE

Everything that passes in London, and everything in the country, breathes a firm and universal determination on the part of the people to obtain the Reform Bill. In the meantime there is no breach of the peace [violent disturbance], and it is our most earnest and anxious hope that all will continue tranquil [peaceful], for nothing would be so likely to establish the Duke of Wellington in power, as disturbances which must be repressed [put down] by force. The troops are drawing near to London on all sides, and the Duke is not a man to spare the sword; but we trust there will be no pretence [excuse] for drawing it. Tremendous meetings continue to be held in all parts of the **metropolis** [London], and in several districts the inhabitants have refused to pay taxes ... if the country continues to manifest [show] the same determined yet peaceable and **constitutional** spirit which was displayed there [in Leeds], we cannot believe that the Duke of Wellington can resist it. He must, sooner or later, retire from the contest.

All England is meeting, yet there is commotion nowhere. There is scarcely a town in this county, or a village in this neighbourhood, where public meetings have not been held, or are not about to be held, for the purpose of **petitioning** the House of Commons ... Where meetings were never held before, they are held now.

The *Leeds Mercury* of 15 May 1832 urges opposition to the Tory leader, the Duke of Wellington, and support for the Reform Bill.

Passing the Bill

Radicals like **Orator** Hunt demanded universal male **suffrage** – votes for all men (no one yet championed votes for women). But the Whig Reform **Bill** was much narrower. It proposed to scrap rotten boroughs, and in effect give the vote to the middle class – the large new propertied class created by the Industrial Revolution.

The Reformers' Attack on the Old Rotten Tree; or, the Foul Nests of the Cormorants in Danger.

Chopping down a rotten tree: the 1832 crisis is reflected in a typical cartoon of the time, with reformers seen destroying the rotten borough system.

Even this was too much for the Tories, representing the traditional landowning classes. Though outvoted in the House of Commons, where the Bill was introduced in March 1831, the Tories had a majority in the **House of Lords** – and at that time laws could only be passed if the Lords were willing. After a long struggle, King William IV agreed that, if necessary, he would create 50 new Whig **peers** (lords) to give the government a majority. The Lords then gave way, and the Bill became law in June 1832.

Evaluation

This passage was part of a leader or editorial, an article expressing the newspaper's views. It appeared in a special issue — an unusual event at the time, described by the paper itself as an 'extraordinary publication ... called for by the extraordinary crisis which has come upon us'. It appeared when the Whig prime minister, Lord Grey, had resigned, after failing in his first attempt to persuade the king to create new **peers**, and the Duke of Wellington was trying to rally support to form a Tory government.

The *Mercury's* article conveys the intense excitement in the country. Representing the point of view of the Yorkshire mill-owners, the paper was strongly in favour of reform. It emphasized popular enthusiasm for the cause, but favoured peaceful, legal action — and obviously feared that 'the Iron Duke' might find an excuse to call in troops and crush the movement by force.

FREEING THE SLAVES

Slavery has existed in many societies. In Britain, it died out in the early Middle Ages. But after the **colonization** of the Americas, Europeans began a profitable trade, buying or kidnapping slaves in West Africa and transporting them across the Atlantic to plantations and other places where a workforce was wanted.

English **merchants** and sailors joined in the trade with enthusiasm. Shackled together, huge numbers of Africans died on the transatlantic voyage, but ports such as Liverpool, Lancaster and Bristol prospered through the slave trade, and quantities of sugar, rum, tobacco, cotton and other raw materials reached Britain in return for slaves who had been purchased for a few manufactured goods. The vile nature of the slave trade only began to be widely recognized towards the end of the 18th century.

Humanitarian Campaigners

In 1772 slavery was declared to be illegal in England itself. Then, from the 1780s, an MP, William Wilberforce, campaigned against the slave trade. He was a **humanitarian** and a leader of the influential **Evangelical** movement. Thanks to Wilberforce and his supporters, Parliament finally abolished the slave trade (but not slavery itself) in 1807.

Colonial Slavery

Mr O'Connell said that the question which the **House [of Commons]** had then to decide was, whether it would give freedom, or continue slavery to 800,000 negroes [black people]. After a long and declamatory speech the hon. gentleman said he hoped that the voice of humanity, common sense, and of justice, would be wafted over the waves of the Atlantic, and would speedily cause the abandonment of this nefarious [evil] system. The British **legislature**, by putting an end to slavery in the **colonies**, would not only do good to their own country, but would prove themselves to be the benefactors of the human race [people who benefit humanity] over the whole world.– (Hear, hear) Let the freedom of the negro be proclaimed in the first instance, and let the question of compensation be afterwards considered, when a proper case was made out for parliament to legislate [make laws] upon. He called on the house at once to give liberty to their fellow creatures – he called on them to throw aside all [self-]interested, all selfish feelings – he called on them to take this step firmly and boldly – he called on them 'to be just and fear not.' – (hear.)

The House of Commons' debate on the Emancipation Bill is reported by the *Manchester Guardian* of 8 June 1833.

Evaluation

From the early 19th century, newspapers published accounts of proceedings in Parliament. Skilled shorthand reporters recorded speeches very accurately, even including approving cries of 'Hear, hear' from supporters. Daniel O'Connell was an Irish national leader and reformer. The *Manchester Guardian* was conservative in outlook at this time, and disliked O'Connell. His speech is described as 'long and declamatory' ('hammy'), though it is fairly typical of the flowery style of 19th-century oratory.

All MPs are 'hon.' (honourable) or 'rt hon.' (right honourable).

Slaves who already lived in Britain's West Indian colonies were still unfree. There was strong resistance to **emancipation** (freeing them), for slaves were worth money and had been legally acquired. After another long campaign, in 1833 slavery was abolished throughout the British Empire, the masters receiving £20 million in compensation. Wilberforce died just a month before the **Act** was passed.

Heroes of the anti-slavery movement. After a lifelong struggle, Wilberforce (centre) died as slavery was about to end.

REFORMING THE BOROUGHS

The Great Reform **Act** of 1832 (page 8) changed the way that Parliament was elected, giving a voice to new sections of the community. But local government was equally in need of **reform**. This was especially true of the boroughs – towns recognized by the grant of a **royal charter** and governed by a **corporation** or town council. Like Parliament before 1832, the boroughs had hardly changed for centuries, so great industrial cities like Birmingham and Manchester had no councils while some existing boroughs had become tiny. And in many cases a corporation was chosen by such small numbers of people that it was able to control elections and stay in office indefinitely. That is why *The Times* described the municipal (borough) corporations as 'self-elected' – a situation that led to the corrupt practices described by the newspaper (below).

Sweeping Changes

The Municipal Corporations Act was passed in 1835. All councils were to be elected by the male ratepayers – that is, men who owned property and paid local taxes. As in the 1832 Reform Act, power and responsibility were restricted to the better-off. Councils had to meet in public so that their views and decisions were known to everyone. Records of tax income and expenditure were to be checked. Sizeable towns without councils were quickly given borough status.

LOCAL CORRUPTION

One of the most important and pressing subjects of solicitude [concern] in the present state of the country has been that of corporation reform. The most active spring [cause] of election bribery and villainy everywhere is known to be the corporation system. The members of corporations throughout England are for the most part self-elected, and wholly irresponsible ... They have contrived ... to oust [deprive] the town inhabitants, for whose benefit the charters were originally granted, of all rights ... They have ... confiscated to their own benefit the funds, of which they were lawfully but **trustees**. There is scarcely an instance of any town sending representatives to Parliament where the mayor, alderman &c [etc.] have not regularly seized upon, or clutched at, the nomination of the members [MPs] ...The fact is, that Parliamentary reform, if it were not to include corporation reform ... would have been literally a dead letter [of no effect].

25 June 1833: *The Times* thunders against corrupt boroughs.

Cause for concern: squalid conditions in many 19th-century cities needed to be tackled by local government, but were too often ignored.

New Councils

The reformed councils were allowed to perform many tasks, such as providing street lighting and supplying clean water. The new councils were more honest than the old ones, but many of them preferred to save money rather than provide services, so major problems remained.

Evaluation

This leading article from *The Times* explains why the newspaper was nicknamed 'the Thunderer'. Though the language used is difficult, the general intention is clear — a tremendous rumbling assault on corruption in the corporations that ran British boroughs. No specific offenders were named, since that might have caused legal difficulties for a paper that was flinging about charges of bribery, 'villainy', and theft or misuse of funds. In any case, details would have weakened *The Times*'s picture of universal corruption.

This was actually unfair to some corporations, which persuaded Parliament to let them provide services for the community. *The Times* would no doubt have argued that its general picture was accurate, and that 'thundering' was essential to make governments sit up and take notice.

THE CHARTIST MOVEMENT

Early in the 19th century, many working-class people supported radicals such as **Orator** Hunt, and later on joined the campaign for the 1832 **Reform Act**. But when it was passed, the Act gave the vote only to people who owned property. Ordinary workers felt disillusioned, especially when the newly reformed Parliament broke up **trade unions** and passed a harsh new Poor Law (page 18).

Resentment intensified from 1836, when hard times brought unemployment and wage cuts. People began to organize and demonstrate, and in 1838 the People's Charter was published. Among its six aims were universal male **suffrage** (votes for all men), the secret ballot (so no one knew who you had voted for), and other measures to secure political equality. Supporters of the Charter became known as Chartists.

Failure or Success?

In 1839 a **petition** was presented to Parliament asking for the Charter to become law. But although huge numbers of people had signed the petition, the **House of Commons** rejected it with scorn. The same happened in 1842 and again in 1848.

CHARTIST RIOTS AT NEWPORT, MONMOUTHSHIRE

Defeat and death of twenty of the rioters — arrest of Mr Frost and other leaders

We this day present the readers of the *Observer* with a very copious account of a serious insurrection [uprising] which has broken out in South Wales. On Monday morning about 9 o'clock a large assemblage [gathering] of Chartists, variously estimated at from 8,000 to 10,000 in number under the leadership of Mr John Frost ... marched into that town with the view of first plundering and then sacking [destroying] it. The **magistrates** ... took the precaution of calling in the aid of about thirty soldiers of the 45th regiment ... They also swore in a great number of special constables, and remained up in the Westgate Hotel ... The Chartists having marched up to the Westgate Hotel, gave three cheers for the Charter, and then, finding that the parties within did not respond ... commenced a general attack upon it ... The military first fired a round over their heads ... The fire of the military was briskly returned by the Chartists, who took possession of the greatest part of the basement storey. But finding that, from the superior position of the troops, they were not likely to dislodge them, and seeing many of their own number fall, killed and wounded at their sides, they relinquished the unequal contest, and retreated to the fields, after a quarter of an hour's engagement.

The *Observer* of 10 November 1839 describes the 'Newport rising' six days earlier.

Evaluation

The *Observer's* readers were middle-class people, unlikely to sympathize with Chartist miners and iron-workers. The paper's hostile account of the 'Newport rising' is not surprising, but it contains interesting contradictions. The event is a 'riot' (a mindless rampage) in one place, but 'a serious insurrection' (a revolutionary uprising) in another. According to the *Observer*, the Chartists intended to plunder and sack the town — like criminals rather than men with a cause.

Some historians think the 'rising' was just a demonstration intended to free some imprisoned Chartists, while others picture it as part of a planned national revolution that was called off everywhere else. Frost, an ex-mayor of Newport, was convicted of treason (a crime against the state) and sentenced to death, but was eventually **transported** to a British **colony**, the island of Tasmania.

Imaginary report: the Chartist rising at Newport, by a contemporary artist. In reality the top-hatted magistrates were safe inside the hotel, and it was the Chartists that were shot down.

One wing of the Chartists believed that, despite setbacks, they would eventually convince Parliament. This 'moral force' wing was opposed by 'physical force' Chartists who believed the use of violence was justified. The split weakened the Chartists, who were faced by a determined Parliament, government and army. Even in 1848, when revolutions swept Europe, Chartist demonstrations achieved nothing, and the movement fizzled out. However, most of the aims for which the Chartists fought were achieved, though some not until 1918.

REFORM OF THE WORKPLACE

Poverty and bad working conditions existed long before the Industrial Revolution. But they were more obvious in the crowded factories and workshops of the 19th century. Men, women and children worked for long hours in health-destroying, dangerous jobs, in factories or underground in mines. There was no time for leisure or money for education, and sick or disabled workers could expect no compensation.

Parliament passed laws to improve conditions from as early as 1802, but effective **reform** campaigns got under way only in the 1830s. As with the anti-slavery movement, many of the leaders were Tories, not normally in favour of reform but moved by **humanitarian** and **Evangelical** Christian beliefs. The most influential of these was Lord Ashley, who later became Earl of Shaftesbury.

Resistance to Reform

Serious reforms began when **Royal Commissions** and parliamentary committees published reports on working conditions. The treatment of women and small children particularly horrified MPs, but resistance to change remained strong. Manufacturers argued that restrictions would damage trade, and many working families opposed reform because their children's earnings helped them to survive.

HOPE FOR OUR COUNTRY

There is no decision to which the **House of Commons** has come, for many years, that has given us so much satisfaction as that decision which affirmed [approved] Lord Ashley's amendment in favour of a Ten Hours' **Bill** for female labourers. With Mr Fielden, we should rather the House had decided upon a gradual approach to eight hours of female labour; but that proposition [proposal] was not before the House. ... Such a decision gives us hope for our country. For some time past it has seemed to us that England was destined to sink under the soul destroying influence of wealth-worship – under the miserable preference of political economy [economic theory] to Christian principle. But, thank God, the decision of Monday night gives us better hope... It is good for England that the political economists have received this decisive defeat – that the principle of legislative [legal] protection for the labourer has achieved this decisive victory.

The *Morning Post* of 20 March 1844 describes the proposed **Factory Act** as a great moral victory.

An image that shocked: this drawing of a half-naked young woman, harnessed like an animal and dragging a waggon underground, was part of an official report that led to the passing of the 1842 Mines Act.

Evaluation

The *Morning Post* spoke for the landowning classes, and had only limited sympathy with manufacturers and businessmen. This partly explains its hostile attitude towards 'wealth worship' and 'political economists' (today we just call them economists), who argued that governments should not interfere with the 'iron laws' of economics, or **market forces**, even for humanitarian reasons.

The newspaper was pleased that the House of Commons had amended (altered) the government's Factory Act by cutting the daily maximum of hours a woman could work to ten, down from the limit of twelve proposed in the Act. The newspaper's rejoicing was short-lived: the government put pressure on MPs and the amendment was reversed. However, John Fielden, the Radical MP mentioned by the *Post*, did carry through a Ten Hours Act in 1847.

Factories and Mines

The Factory Act of 1833 was an important landmark. Children under nine could no longer be employed, and hours of work for young people were limited: to 48 hours a week if you were between nine and thirteen, and to 69 hours if you were between thirteen and nineteen. New curbs were introduced in the Mines Act (1842) and a further Factory Act (1844). But the reformers' goal – a maximum ten-hour day for women and children – was not achieved until 1847. Further reforms followed, but even in 1901 children of twelve could leave school and take jobs.

INTO THE WORKHOUSE

In the 19th century, 'poor relief' described the help given to people who could not support themselves. There were no **state pensions** or other **welfare benefits**, so the old, the sick and the unemployed were all at risk. Poor relief was provided by local government – the **parish** authorities, who raised money by local taxation (the poor rate).

Those who needed relief, known as paupers, were taken into specially built workhouses ('indoor relief'), or were allowed to live in their own homes ('outdoor relief') while receiving help. As the name suggests, inmates of workhouses might have to perform some kind of labour. By the 19th century, loopholes in the outdoor relief system, exploited by employers, had made it very expensive.

The New Poor Law

It is impossible not to be struck with the frightful mortality [loss of life] which appears to be the result of the administration of the New Poor Law. For the last month (we can personally testify) not a week has elapsed [passed] without the disclosure of some heartrending case, either of 'death from destitution' [utter poverty] out of the Workhouse or of gross 'neglect of medical attendance' in it. Does it not sound horrible?

Yet we repeat that each week brings its two or three cases (reported in **metropolitan** papers alone) of human beings perishing through lack of necessities of life [food and shelter], or the necessary attendance [medical help] in disease. An infant refused medical attention in one town, and dying in its mother's arms as she was bearing it to another. A poor labourer, living for weeks on potatoes or dry bread, sleeping in a straw loft like a dog, and dying at last rather than go to the Workhouse, which he had once entered and remembered but to dread. Another literally starving, with a starving wife and four starving children, denied relief in or out of the house ... actually (so the jury found) dying of disease and hunger in consequence.

A Cruel Form of Help

The reforming Poor Law Amendment **Act** (1834) was influenced by a belief – typical of the time – that working people should be less idle and more self-reliant. The Act ended outdoor relief for able-bodied (fit) people. If they became paupers and wanted relief, they must go into the workhouse.

Ten years after its passing, the working of the New Poor Law is condemned by the *News of the World* of 15 December 1844.

Husbands and wives, and parents and children, were separated, and conditions in workhouses were made deliberately unpleasant, so that inmates would leave if they possibly could. But many people became unemployed and paupers through no fault of their own. The evils of the 'New Poor Law' were often denounced, and 'the workhouse' became a symbol of shame and suffering – in spite of which the system was not changed for over 80 years.

Life in the workhouse: this photo shows women at St Pancras in London. The atmosphere is still grim, though the picture was taken around 1900.

Evaluation

Founded in 1843, the *News of the World* was one of the publications that benefited when the abolition of stamp duty (a tax) on newspapers made them cheaper and wider in their appeal. It was aimed at a larger, less wealthy and privileged readership than established newspapers such as *The Times*.

Like later mass-market publications, it used brief but effective personal stories to make its points. The shame and lack of dignity of workhouse life is illustrated by the example of a labourer who preferred to die rather than become an inmate. The danger of using personal stories in this way is that they might not be typical and can be used to paint a biased picture; but in the case of the Poor Law, there is abundant evidence to support the *News of the World's* stand.

THE FREE TRADE ERA

For a long time, governments believed that home-produced goods should be protected from foreign competition. Goods from abroad were subjected to taxes (called duties or tariffs) to make them more expensive than home-produced goods. But by the 19th century, economists argued that this system (protectionism) should be scrapped in favour of **Free Trade**. They argued that abolishing tariffs and allowing free competition would lead to greater efficiency and lower prices.

In Britain, the Corn Laws, introduced in 1815, were especially unpopular. Intended to protect farmers, they allowed only limited amounts of foreign grain into the country unless British-produced grain became very scarce. The Corn Laws were unpopular with working people because they kept up the price of bread, the food basic to survival.

TOTAL REPEAL OF THE CORN LAWS

It appears to be at length pretty certain that the end of the Corn Laws is rapidly approaching, and the question now is, who dealt them the fatal blow? There need not, however, be much doubt about the matter. To have watched the progress of events for the last seven or eight years, and not to be able to fix with certainty on the author of this assassination, seems to us scarcely a conceivable predicament [hardly imaginable]; and yet *The Times* asks the question. Many circumstances, and many men have, we admit, concurred [run together] in bringing us to the point at which we have now arrived. The Tory ministers have done something, the Liberal ex-ministers have done more; but the great agent in the business has been the Anti-Corn Law League. No one in his senses can deny this. Without the kind assistance of the League, the Corn Laws would, probably, have perished some day or another, because it is not in the nature of injustice to be everlasting; but we much fear they would have outlived the present generation, and sent many thousands and tens of thousands prematurely [before their time] to their graves.

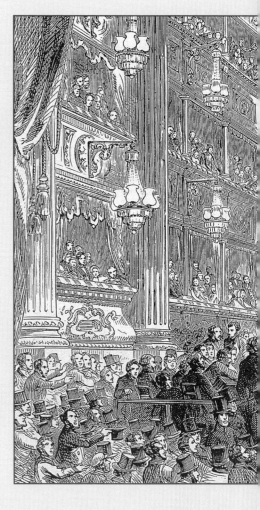

The *Sunday Times* of 7 December 1845 comments on the approaching repeal of the Corn Laws.

Repeal of the Corn Laws

Industrialists also disliked the Corn Laws, since foreign countries hit back by taxing British manufacturers. And cheaper bread meant low wage bills (employees would not have to be paid so much for them to be able to live) and a better-fed, more contented workforce. Landowners, however, argued that it was vital to protect British agriculture. As the 'landed interest' was still strong in Parliament, change seemed unlikely.

In 1838 the Anti-Corn Law League was founded in Manchester. Led by two Northern MPs, Richard Cobden and John Bright, the League strongly influenced public opinion by using mass meetings, the new railway network and the new, cheap national post to spread its message. In 1846 the prime minister, Sir Robert Peel, finally decided to repeal (cancel) the Corn Laws, and the Free Trade era began.

Mass-meeting, 1843: the Anti-Corn Law League assembles in Drury Lane Theatre, London. The League was a spectacularly successful example of a pressure group.

EDUCATION FOR THE MASSES

Before the 19th century, there were no state-provided schools and poor children seldom received an education. Early efforts were made by religious individuals and societies. Once a week, Sunday Schools gave children a few hours' instruction. Some schools were built and run by two voluntary societies, one Anglican (Church of England) and the other Nonconformist (non-Anglican Protestant).

The first, timid step towards government involvement was taken in 1833, when Parliament gave the religious societies a grant of £20,000 towards building more schools. A few years later, the grant increased and inspectors were appointed to supervise the way it was spent. But little more was done, except by the **factory reformer** Lord Shaftesbury, who set up 'ragged schools' to educate the very poorest children.

To the editor of the *Manchester Guardian*

Sir

I visited 102 houses in the neighbourhood of Deansgate, and found that there were only 84 children attending day schools, against 127, between 3 and 15, who were neither at day school nor at work. The **statistical society** finds, in the southern part of the district ... that 148 children are attending day schools, while 232, over 3 years old are neither at day schools nor at work ... It is only about a seventh part of the Deansgate district, and is probably as fair an average specimen of ... the more densely-peopled parts of Manchester and Salford as could have been selected. The chief interest, therefore, of the report arises from the fact that it represents the condition of far more than a quarter of a million of people ... Is it not time that something should be done, or be preparing to be done, to remedy the vast evil? Are we not sufficiently convinced that to educate these masses would be wiser and more economical than to build workhouses, and prisons, and **reformatories** for them? But some will, perhaps, say that parents of the lowest class will not send their children to school even when schools are provided. Then, I reply, so much the more need of legislation, and of some comprehensive measures which shall grapple with neglect and indolence [laziness]. If we were in earnest, many things might be done.

EB Brotherton

The Road to Reform

In 1860, three-quarters of British children still received no schooling. Yet industrial progress was creating a demand for people with technical skills or at least basic literacy. Pressure was building up to give more people the vote, which made it more urgent to educate future voters.

New **pressure groups** were formed to argue for a national system of compulsory education, and a beginning was made at last in 1870. The voluntary societies were not replaced, but became part of a larger system. Where they could not provide enough schools, local people could elect a school board and build and maintain a school out of the rates (local taxes).

By 1899 'elementary education' –

A letter from EB Brotherton, published in the *Manchester Guardian* of 6 September 1864.

Elementary education: free, compulsory, and, at this date (1893), quite basic. These girls at a Board School are being taught how to be good housewives, still seen as their main role in life.

basic education – was free and compulsory for children between five and twelve. Secondary education had to wait until the new century arrived.

Evaluation

In the 19th century, readers' letters began to be regularly published in newspapers. This was one outlet for public opinion — at any rate, the opinion of educated and leisured people. Papers published a variety of views, although they inevitably favoured letters that supported their own outlook.

However, correspondents sometimes exposed scandals or abuses. A writer such as EB Brotherton, whose letter appears opposite, practised what we should now call 'investigative journalism'. The letters he published in the *Manchester Guardian* resembled well-researched newspaper articles of a type that was still relatively rare in 1864, exposing current abuses. Brotherton's dry statistics, revealing that most children in a large city had no chance of a basic education, made an impact. Described as 'the thunderclap from the North', his investigations strengthened calls for Parliament to act.

THE NATION'S HEALTH

Problems of **sanitation**, pollution and disease became far more serious during the Industrial Revolution. In the rapidly growing cities, there were no organized arrangements for providing clean water, disposing of sewage, or cleansing filth from the streets. Many families were forced into overcrowded slum houses – unsafe, unhealthy buildings – which lacked toilets or drains. Conditions in their workplaces were also often horribly unhealthy. Factories belched smoke into the atmosphere, coating surrounding areas with soot. Industrial premises, workshops, chemical plants and slaughter-houses emptied their waste products into rivers or on to city dumps. London's sewage was discharged into the River Thames, which provided Londoners with their water supply.

CLEANSE THE CITIES!

Not a day too soon, the General Board of Health has published its directions and regulations against the impending pest [cholera] ... nobody can doubt that the disease is near and may suddenly appear, and number its weekly thousands, as it did four years ago ...Whatever has been done in the interval by way of sewerage can scarcely have kept pace with the immense increase of population, and what has been done to improve the habitations [dwellings] of the poor has been confined to a few **model lodginghouses**, while, as a general rule, the working classes are more crowded every year ... We could certainly wish that the 'directions' and 'regulations' before us were rather more simple and intelligible. Perhaps, some gentleman could be found in the office of the Board of Health competent to translate the document from Parliamentary English to that in common use ... we fear that even this formidable docu-ment will prove utterly ineffectual [not effective] ... Thoroughfares [public ways] ... dwelling houses, drains, and all receptacles of filth [cesspits], come under the ban of the board, and the proper authorities are urged to inspect and to cleanse them; but a man may go on boiling wagonloads of putrid fat in the midst of a dense population, without even a shaft [chimney] to carry off the vapour, or may boil festering bones, and keep them by hundreds of tons over human dwellings ... and there will be no remedy against him.

Not surprisingly, epidemics of **cholera**, **typhoid** and other dread diseases swept the country at various times throughout the 19th century.

The Struggle for Reform

Official reports and the threat of a new cholera epidemic led to the passing of the first Public Health **Act** in 1848. Local authorities were allowed – not compelled – to set up boards of health and appoint medical officers. Some towns made great improvements, but there was considerable resistance to spending local money and interfering with business practices even if these created an unhealthy environment.

Health anxieties are voiced by _The Times_ on 22 September 1853.

Evaluation

This leader from *The Times* suggests the dread inspired in the 19th century by cholera, which was believed to have killed 10,000 Londoners during the previous outbreak in 1848–9. By the 1850s *The Times* had become quite conservative, and it might have been expected to protest against 'directions and regulations' as the work of government busybodies. Instead, faced with the threat of a cholera epidemic which had already reached Newcastle, its only complaints were that the directions had been issued 'not a day too soon' (at the last moment), and that they were written in a way that was hard to understand — a remark made many times, before and since, about official publications.

The article gives a lively description of city workshops whose polluting and health-threatening activities were still not subject to legal penalties.

Progress was slow, but bit by bit Parliament passed the necessary laws. London's magnificently engineered sewers were constructed with great speed after 'the Great Stink' of 1858, when the stench from the Thames drove MPs out of Parliament! In the 1870s, local councils were given more duties, including **slum clearance**. By 1900, many eyesores and evil smells had been removed, but serious problems remained.

DIPHTHERIA.   SCROFULA.   CHOLERA.

FATHER THAMES INTRODUCING HIS OFFSPRING TO THE FAIR CITY OF LONDON.

(A Design for a Fresco in the New Houses of Parliament.)

Filth and disease from the river: aiming its satire at Parliament, which stands beside the Thames, the magazine *Punch* pictures the diseases as the river's children.

NEW POLITICAL REFORMS

The Great **Reform Act** of 1832 (page 8) gave the vote to the middle class who had been made richer by the Industrial Revolution. Most MPs believed that possessing property was what gave men the right to take part in politics. So in Parliament there was little pressure for further reform. Outside Parliament, the Chartist movement failed (page 14), and the Anti-Corn Law League (page 20), with its promise of cheap bread, became the new popular cause.

By this time, Britain was forging ahead as the world's greatest industrial and trading nation. Many people still lived in great poverty, but substantial numbers of working-class families did become much better off. The immediate effect was to dampen radical political activity. But in the long run the case for **enfranchising** (giving the vote to) 'respectable' householders was strengthened.

GREAT REFORM DEMONSTRATION AT GLASGOW

On Tuesday the greatest public demonstration that has occurred in Glasgow for many years took place. A large procession, estimated at 30,000 persons, was formed on the Green, and marched through the principal streets and back again, where six platform meetings were held simultaneously, and three resolutions in favour of Reform were carried unanimously at each platform. The first resolution ... pledged the meeting to 'support the Scotch National Reform League in its efforts to obtain by all lawful means registered residential manhood **suffrage**...'

Mr John Bright, MP, who had accepted an invitation to address the inhabitants of Glasgow at an evening meeting, witnessed the progress of the procession from the window of the Cobden Hotel in Argyle Street. As the procession and the immense crowd which accompanied it passed by the hotel repeated cheers were given for Mr Bright.

Votes for Working Men

In 1866 economic troubles and rioting helped to revive the reform issue. In 1867 the Conservatives put through the Second Reform Act which enfranchised skilled workers in the cities.

Other political reforms followed. The Ballot Act of 1872 introduced voting in secret. This meant that a man need no longer fear to lose his job if he voted differently from his employer.

The reform movement in action, as reported by the *Observer* on 21 October 1866.

Rally for reform, May 1867: a large crowd assembles in London's Hyde Park to demand the vote. Such meetings helped to bring about the Second Reform Act.

A third Reform Act in 1884 enfranchised prosperous workers in rural areas.

These 19th-century advances still left a majority of adults without the vote – all women, and about a third of men. Justice was done to them only in the 20th century.

Evaluation

The article provides an interesting snapshot of Victorian manners and public politics. Such a mass meeting would have alarmed governments and local authorities earlier, in the Peterloo period. By the 1860s it had become thoroughly respectable, with platform meetings (crowds gathered round speakers on a platform in a hall or the open air), speeches and a procession past the hotel of Radical MP John Bright. The resolutions passed were reported by the *Observer* without any hint of disapproval.

The reform demanded was also consciously respectable – basically votes for adult men with fixed, officially registered addresses ('registered residential manhood suffrage'). Exceptionally large numbers took part in the demonstration or came along to watch, but public meetings of all sorts were well attended in this period, before radio and TV provided alternative sources of information and entertainment. However, even today mass demonstrations and marches still take place when people become aroused by important issues.

WOMEN'S RIGHTS

Throughout history and in most societies, women have had fewer rights than men, and have spent their lives under male control. In early 19th-century Britain their legal status was similar to the status of children: decisions about how and where they lived were made for them, and if they were married their property and earnings belonged to their husbands. Few girls went to school, and the universities and most professions were closed to them. Many poor women had to work in factories, or as servants or governesses (teachers of children in private households), but home-making and child-bearing were considered the 'natural' career choices for a woman.

Advances and Opportunities

But the 19th century did bring important advances. Pioneering girls' schools and colleges were opened and, under the 1870 Act (page 22), girls as well as boys received an elementary education. Some universities awarded degrees to women, and medical schools were opened to them. New job opportunities also appeared, although many professions remained closed and women were generally poorly paid.

The legal position of women also improved in the course of time. A series of Married Women's Property **Acts** gave wives control over their property and earnings. The divorce laws, which had favoured men, were made somewhat less unjust. Women were allowed to vote in local elections and even to become councillors. Yet the right to vote in elections for Parliament, or to become MPs, was still refused, and would only be gained in the following century.

WOMEN'S PROPERTY — AND MEN'S

On Monday last there came into operation a statute [law] known as the Married Woman's Property Act, but which may be more correctly described as an act for the better protection of husbands. For a long time past it has been a complaint with a certain number of ladies who have taken upon themselves the championship of their sex that ... the property of the wife ... becomes the property of the husband, and liable for his debts. They forgot to take into account the fact that the credit of the husband was the property of his wife, and that she could pledge it to any extent, and leave him to endure the consequences ... As to what may ultimately be its general effect upon society and upon our domestic relations, we should prefer to reserve our opinion. Many women have been pillaged and robbed by their husbands. But it is equally certain that many husbands have been ruined by the extravagance of their wives. ... In any case, the advocates of woman's rights have got an instalment of their demands, and it is to be hoped that they will be satisfied.

The *Observer* of 7 January 1883 comments on the passing of the Married Woman's Property Act.

Evaluation

The extract is taken from a long editorial commenting on the newly-passed Married Women's Property Act, which gave wives control of their own property and earnings. The *Observer* article contains a type of writing about women that would continue to be seen well into the 20th century. It is jokey in tone, as though the issues dealt with by the Act were rather trivial. Deliberately ignoring the principle of equal rights that was being established, it argued that husbands would be the ones to benefit from the Act because they would no longer be responsible for their extravagant wives' debts!

You would find it a useful exercise to analyze the extract for its loaded use of language and its debatable facts. For example, 'taken upon themselves' implies that the ladies are saucily claiming to speak for 'their sex'. But are they behaving differently from other campaigners, including newspapers? And is it really 'equally certain that many husbands have been ruined by the extravagance of their wives'?

The Divorce Court, 1870, a time when the law was unjust in being harder on women's faults in marriage than on men's. Note that all the court officials are male.

TIMELINE

1815 — End of the wars against France. British industry depressed. Corn Laws passed to protect agriculture

1819 — Peterloo massacre

1830 — Lord Grey becomes prime minister of a Whig government

1832 — Great Reform Bill gives the middle classes the right to vote

1833 — Abolition of slavery in the British Empire. First effective Factory Act. First government grant for education

1834 — The Poor Law Amendment Act establishes a harsh system of poor relief

1835 — The Municipal Corporations Act reforms the boroughs

1837 — Queen Victoria comes to the throne

1839 — First Chartist petition for universal male suffrage rejected by Parliament. The Newport rising by Chartists is suppressed

1842 — Second Chartist petition rejected. Mines Act regulates working hours and conditions underground

1844 — A new Factory Act shortens maximum working hours

1846 — Repeal of the Corn Laws. Beginning of the Free Trade era

1847 — 'Ten Hour' Act limits working hours further

1848 — First Public Health Act. Failure of the final Chartist petition and Chartist demonstration in London

1867 — Second Reform Act gives the vote to skilled workers

1870 — Education Act introduces measures for universal elementary education

1872 — Ballot Act introduces voting in secret

1882 — Married Women's Property Act gives women control over their own property and earnings

1884 — Third Reform Act gives the vote to many rural workers

GLOSSARY

ACT: An Act of Parliament – that is, a law made by Parliament.

BILL: A proposed Act of Parliament. A Bill becomes an ACT when the Commons, Lords and Crown have all approved it.

CHOLERA: A dangerous disease caused by consuming infected food or water.

COLONIZATION: The process of establishing a COLONY.

COLONY: A territory ruled by an outside power (plural: **colonies**). Britain possessed many colonies in the West Indies, Africa and elsewhere.

CONSTITUTIONAL: To do with a country's fundamental political arrangments.

CORPORATION: A body that is incorporated – that is, officially recognized, like the council running a borough.

EMANCIPATION: Liberation from slavery or inferior status.

ENFRANCHISE (someone): To give the right to vote to (someone).

EPIDEMIC DISEASES: Diseases that spread rapidly, affecting many people.

EVANGELICAL: One of a group within the Church of England with a strong commitment to missionary work and HUMANITARIAN causes.

FACTORY REFORMER: Person who worked to have laws passed improving conditions in the factories.

FREE TRADE: Trade between nations that is not hindered by tariffs – taxes imposed by governments on foreign goods.

HOUSE OF COMMONS: The elected 'lower house' in Parliament.

HOUSE OF LORDS: The non-elected 'upper house' of Parliament, most of whose members (peers) inherited their titles and their right to sit in the House.

HUMANITARIAN: Person with sympathy for fellow-humans. Applied to reformers whose main object was to relieve suffering.

INDUSTRIALIST: Person running an industrial (manufacturing) business.

LEGISLATURE: Law-making body. In Britain this means Parliament.

MAGISTRATE: A public officer, especially a local judge; often used to describe justices of the peace, who also carried out some local government duties.

MARKET FORCES: The operation of supply and demand to fix prices (including wages – the 'price' of labour) when these forces are not modified by (for example) laws and regulations.

MERCHANT: A person who makes money through buying commodities and selling them at a profit.

METROPOLIS: A large city (adjective: **metropolitan**). Often used to mean London.

MODEL LODGINGHOUSE: A home or hostel offering high-quality accommodation and regarded as a model (good example) for other landlords.

ORATOR: A speech-maker. Oratory is the art of making speeches. Usually these words are used when the speech is eloquent or flowery.

PARISH: A small local government district (originally the area served by a church).

PEERS: Members of the HOUSE OF LORDS.

PETITION: A written request, usually a document signed by large numbers of people.

PETITIONING: Presenting a PETITION.

PRESSURE GROUP: A group working together to put pressure on the government for a particular purpose.

REFORM: A change in the law, or in the way something is organized, in order to remove abuses or bring about improvements.

REFORMATORIES: Places to which young people were sent after being convicted of a crime.

REFORMING MOVEMENT: A group of association of people who are trying to bring about REFORM.

ROYAL CHARTER: A document issued by the monarch, granting certain rights, for example to a town.

ROYAL COMMISSION: A government-appointed body, usually including experts, set up to investigate a problem.

SANITATION: Conditions that promote health and prevent disease, particularly concerning drains and sewage.

SLUM CLEARANCE: Knocking down slums (unsafe, unhealthy groups of buildings).

STATE PENSIONS: Regular payments made by the state to people who have stopped working, notably Old Age Pensions, first introduced in Britain in 1908.

STATISTICAL SOCIETY: An organization devoted to gathering statistics – figures giving an exact account of a situation, for example the number of children attending schools.

SUFFRAGE: The right to vote.

TRADE UNION: An association of workers, formed to press for better wages and conditions.

TRANSPORTED: Sent to a COLONY overseas as a convict.

TRUSTEE: A person who has responsibility for the safe-keeping of something that does not belong to them, such as land or money.

TYPHOID: More correctly, typhoid fever: a dangerous disease caused by consuming infected food or water.

WELFARE BENEFITS: Payments and other forms of help, given by the state to people who are sick, unemployed, old, or in need.

YEOMANRY: A volunteer, part-time cavalry force, raised for national defence – or, as at 'Peterloo', to maintain order or put down discontent.

RESOURCES

Books

Chamberlin, ER, *Everyday Life in Victorian Times*, 1993, Simon & Schuster

Macdonald, F, *Women in 19th century Europe*, 1999, Belitha Press

Milton, B, *A Victorian Mill*, 1994, Watts

Morris, N, *Life in Victorian Times: Home and School*, 1999, Belitha Press

Morris, N, *Life in Victorian Times: Work and Industry*, 1999, Belitha Press

Rees, R, *Victorians at School*, 1995, Heinemann

Wood, R, *A Victorian Street*, 1993, Wayland

Deary, T, *The Vile Victorians*, 1994, Scholastic

Farman, J, *History in a Hurry: Victorians*, 1997, Macmillan

Video cassettes

Victorian Britain, 1999, Castle Home Video.

Websites

'The Victorian Web':
www.victorianweb.org/victorian/history/sochistov.html

Visit www.learn.co.uk, the award-winning educational website backed by the *Guardian*, for exciting historical resources and online events.

Places to visit

Many 19th-century buildings are still standing, and most local museums have displays, sometimes with working machinery, etc. The places listed below are a selection, particularly relevant to the topics described in this book. They often feature real or reconstructed environments and interesting activities.

Black Country Museum, Dudley, West Midlands

Coldharbour Mill Working Wool Museum, Devon

The Engineerium, Hove, Sussex

Haig Colliery Mining Museum, Whitehaven, Cumbria

Industrial Museum, Bradford, Yorkshire

Ironbridge Valley of Inventions, Shropshire. This big site has Coalbrookdale Museum of Iron, Blists Hill Victorian Town, and other attractions.

National Coal Mining Museum for England, Wakefield, West Yorkshire

North of England Open Air Museum, Beamish, County Durham

Ragged School Museum, Copperfield Road, East London

Shambellie House Museum, Dumfriesshire

Town Docks Museum, Hull

Welsh Industrial and Maritime Museum, Cardiff

Wollaton Park Industrial Museum, Nottingham

INDEX

Anti-Corn Law League 20-21, 26
Ashley, Lord (see Shaftesbury, Lord)

Ballot Act (1872) 26
boroughs 8, 12-13
Bright, John 21, 26, 27
Brotherton, EB 22-23

Chartism 14-15, 26
child labour 5, 16-17
cholera 24-25
Cobden, Richard 21
colonies 10-11
Conservative Party 5, 21, 26
Corn Laws 20-21
corporations 12-13

disease 5, 24-25
divorce laws 28, 29

education 22-23, 28
Emancipation Bill 10-11
emancipation of slaves 10-11
Evangelical Movement 10

Factory Act (1833) 16, 17
Factory Act (1844) 16, 17
female labour 16-17
Fielden, John 16, 17
Free Trade 5, 20-21
Frost, John 14-15

General Board of Health 24
'Great Stink' 25
Grey, Lord 9

House of Commons 8, 9, 10, 14, 16, 17
House of Lords 9
humanitarian campaigners 10-11
Hunt, Henry 'Orator' 6, 8, 14

'indoor relief' 18
Industrial Revolution 4-5, 6, 8, 16, 24, 26
investigative journalism 23
Irish famine 21

Leeds Mercury 8-9
Liberal Party 5, 20

living conditions 5, 24-25
local government reform 12-13

Manchester Guardian 10-11, 22-23
Married Woman's Property Act 28-29
media 4
middle classes, growth of 5, 8, 26
Mines Act (1842) 17
Morning Post 16-17
Municipal Corporations Act (1835) 12

Napoleonic Wars 6
New Poor Law (see Poor Law Amendment Act)
Newport rising 14-15
News of the World 18-19
newspaper editorial 8-9
newspaper leader (see newspaper editorial)

Observer 14-15, 26-27, 28-29
O'Connell, Daniel 10-11
'outdoor relief' 18

parish authorities 18
parliamentary committees 16
parliamentary reform 8-9
Peel, Sir Robert 5, 21
peers 9
People's Charter 14-15
Peterloo Massacre 6-7
political parties 5
pollution 5, 24-25
Poor Law Amendment Act (New Poor Law) 14, 18-19
poor rate 18
poor relief 18-19
poverty 5, 14, 18-19, 24-25, 26
protectionism 20
public health 24-25
Public Health Act (1848) 24

Radicals 5, 17
ragged schools 22
Reform Bill (Great Reform Act) (1832) 8-9, 12, 14, 26
religious societies 22
'rotten boroughs' 8-9

Royal Charter 12
royal commissions 16

school boards 22
Scotch National Reform League 26
Second Reform Act (1867) 26-27
secret ballot 14, 26
slave trade 10-11
Shaftesbury, Lord 16, 22
slums 24-25
statistical societies 22
Sunday schools 22
Sunday Times 20-21

Ten Hours Act (1847) 16, 17
Third Reform Act (1884) 26
Times, The 6-7 , 12-13, 19, 24-25
Tory Party 5, 6, 8, 9, 16, 20
town councils (see corporations)
trade unions 14
Tyas, John 7
typhoid 24

unemployment 5, 6, 19

voluntary societies 22
voting rights 6, 8-9, 14-15, 26-27, 28

Wellington, Duke of 6, 8, 9
Whigs 5, 8, 9
Wilberforce, William 10-11
William IV, King 9
women's rights 27, 28-29
workhouses 18-19
working conditions 5, 16-17
workplace, reform of 16-17